You've got a friend™

Compiled by
Dan Zadra

Designed by
Kobi Yamada and Steve Potter

COM·PEN´·DI·UM™
Incorporated

Publishing and Communications
Seattle, Washington

Acknowledgements

These quotations were gathered lovingly but unscientifically over several years and/or were contributed by many friends or acquaintances. Some arrived—and survived in our files—on scraps of paper and may therefore be imperfectly worded or attributed. To the authors, contributors and original sources, our thanks, and where appropriate, our apologies. —The Editors.

With Special Thanks to

Jay Baird, Justi Baumgardt, Neil Beaton, Hal Belmont, Beth Bingham, Cate Bradshaw, Doug Cruickshank, Jim Darragh, Josie and Rob Estes, Dawn Ewing, Jennifer Hurwitz, Dick Kamm, Beth Keane, Liam Lavery, Teri O'Brien, Janet Potter & Family, Diane Roger, Robert & Val Yamada, Tote Yamada, Anne Zadra, Augie & Rosie Zadra and August & Arline Zadra.

Credits

Compiled by Dan Zadra

Designed by Kobi Yamada and Steve Potter

ISBN: 1-888387-19-X

Printed in Hong Kong

Thoughts to Celebrate the Joy of Friendship

In Appreciation of My Good Friends

❀

I love you for the part of me that you bring out.
I love you for putting your hand into my heaped-up heart,
and passing over all the foolish and frivolous and weak
things which you cannot help dimly seeing there, and
for drawing out into the light all the beautiful, radiant
belongings, that no one else had looked quite far enough
to find.

I love you for ignoring the possibilities of the fool
and weakling in me, and for laying firm hold on the
possibilities of good in me. I love you for closing your
eyes to the discords in me, and for adding to the music
in me by worshipful listening.

❀

$\mathscr{I}$ love you because you're helping me to make of the lumber of my life not a tavern but a Temple, and of the words of my every day not a reproach but a song. I love you because you have done more than any creed could have done to make me good, and more than any fate could have done to make me happy.

$\mathscr{Y}$ou have done it just by being yourself. Perhaps that is what being a friend means after all.

$\mathscr{F}$riendship?

Yes, please.

Charles Dickens

There is no such thing
as common friendship.

Kelly Ann Rothaus

❀

One does not make friends.
One recognizes them.

Irene Dunn

❀

People come into your life
for a reason, a season or a lifetime.
When you figure out which it is,
you know exactly what to do.

Michelle Venter

Some friendships
are created by nature,
some by interest,
and some by souls.

Jeremy Taylor

❋

Who shall explain
the extraordinary instinct that tells us,
perhaps after a single meeting, that this
or that particular person in some
mysterious way matters to us?

A. C. Benson

How can it be, except by the
miracle of friendship, that someone
can know you so well even though
you have told him virtually
nothing about your life?

Carlos Menta

❋

Love is blind.
Friendship is clairvoyant.

Philippe Soupault

9

A friend is someone
who reaches for your hand...
and touches your heart.

Unknown

❋

*W*hat comes from the heart,
goes to the heart.

Samuel Taylor Coleridge

❋

*F*riendship blossoms when
two people say to each other,
in effect: "What? You too?
I thought I was the only one!"

C. S. Lewis

The friend
given to you by circumstances
over which you have no control
was God's own gift.

Frederick Robertson

✽

Long sought,
rarely found,
and forever kept.

True Friends

When you're with a friend,
your heart has come home.

Emily Farrar

❊

Oh, the comfort, the inexpressible
comfort of feeling safe with a person,
having neither to weigh thoughts nor
measure words but to pour them all out,
just as it is, chaff and grain together,
knowing that a faithful hand will take
and sift them, keeping what is worth
keeping, and then, with the breath
of kindness, blow the rest away.

George Eliot

12

A friend is what
the heart needs all the time.
Henry Van Dyke

❀

*O*ne good heart
attracts another. Each true friend
deserves the other.
Shaker saying

❀

*I*t is the friendship of good people
that is friendship most of all.
Aristotle

*E*ach person represents
a world in us, a world possibly
not born until they arrive, and
it is only by this meeting that
a new world is born.

Anaïs Nin

✿

*I*t was the excitement
of making a new best friend—
the best, the purest feeling
I've ever known.

Keith Hale

Friendship is
a great place.
I'm glad we're here.

Cat Davis

❀

Whatever
souls are made of—
yours and mine
are the same.

Emily Brontë

❀

"Friend...GOOD!"

Frankenstein's monster

*M*y fondest
memories are of
my friends.

Tote Yamada

*R*emembering is
a dream that comes in waves.

Helga Sandburg

❃

*I*n my heart are all the
treasures that I shall ever own:
they are the memories of all
the old friends I have known.

Kimberly Knutsen

❃

I trace my roots,
not to my ancestors, but
to my childhood friends.

Carlos Mento

I don't remember how
we happened to meet each other,
I don't remember who got along with
whom first. All I can remember is
all of us together, always.

The Friendship Page

❋

*T*here has always been,
and there will probably always be,
the three of us crashing through life
together—thick and thin. Our parents
use to call us the "wrecktangle."

Lorna Greene

*W*e set off for school side by side, our feet in step, not touching but feeling as if we were joined at the shoulder, hip, ankle, not to mention heart.

Jamaica Kincaid

❀

*Y*ou know how kids choose up sides for kickball. Well, Jerry Elliot was probably the first and only kid who ever picked me first. Thirty years later we're still great friends.

Frank Blass

So we just wandered off along the path behind the school. We really weren't going anywhere, but when we felt like running, we just ran. The day was like that, and the things we did just happened. And somehow, that made them seem more special—like something from a dream...

Zilpha Keatley Snyder

❀

My parents would only allow brown bread and low-fat margarine in the house. On summer days, my best friends and I would sneak loaves of stark white Wonder Bread, toast it all up and slather it with real butter.

Deborah Snow

We were so naive as kids that
we used to sneak behind the barn
and do nothing.

Johnny Carson

❋

We have a special bond. We're the
only two left in our circle of childhood
pals who haven't had breast implants.

Phoebe Whorley

❋

Time—our youth—it never really goes,
does it? It is all held in our minds.

Helen Santmyer

Never lose your child's heart.
Mencius

❀

I was wise enough
to never grow up while fooling
most people into believing I had.
Margaret Mead

❀

It is not that we belong to the past,
but that the past belongs to us.
Mary Antin

What people
need is a good
listening to.

Mary Lou Casey

*F*riends are those rare people
who ask how we are, and then
wait to hear the answer.

Ed Cunningham

❀

*T*here is a definite process
by which one makes people
into friends, and it involves talking
to them and listening to them
for hours at a time.

Rebecca West

The soul selects
her own society.

Emily Dickinson

❀

A soul friend is someone
with whom we can share our
greatest joys and deepest fears,
confess our worst sins and most
persistent faults, clarify our
highest hopes and perhaps
most unarticulated dreams.

Edward C. Sellner

$\mathcal{S}$omething we were
withholding made us weak…
Until we found it was ourselves.

Robert Frost

❀

$\mathcal{C}$ut out those
intimate little dinners for two—
unless there's someone with you.

Joey Adams

❀

$\mathcal{H}$appiness is not perfected
until it is shared.

Jane Porter

God, I've been starving
for this kind of conversation!

Eleanor Coppola

❁

There was no way for me
to understand it at the time,
but the talk that filled the kitchen
those afternoons served as therapy,
the cheapest kind available to my mother
and her friends. But more than therapy,
that freewheeling, wide-ranging,
exuberant talk functioned as an
outlet for the tremendous creative
energy they possessed.

Paula Marshall

*E*veryone old enough to
have a secret is entitled to have
some special people to keep it with.

Sarah Baker

❋

*T*he silver friend knows
your present, and the gold friend
knows all your past dirt and glories.
Once in a blue moon there's someone
who knows it all, someone who knows
and accepts you unconditionally,
someone who's there for life.

Jill McCorkle

*E*ventually, it's the silences
which make the real conversations
between friends. Not the saying,
but the never needing to say.

Margaret Lee Runbeck

❋

*T*here's no need to say,
"It's been a great day" when
we say good-bye. We just wave
a hand and we understand.

Reminiscence

*I*f somebody
believes in you,
and you believe in your dreams,
it can happen.

Tiffany Bangs

*T*here comes that mysterious
meeting in life when someone
acknowledges who we are and what
we can be, igniting the circuits
of our highest potential.

Rusty Berkus

❀

*M*y best friend is
the one who brings out
the best in me.

Henry Ford

❀

*A*nything, everything, little or big
becomes an adventure when
the right person shares it.

Kathleen Norris

31

*W*e are so much less
without each other.

Leo Buscaglia

❀

*W*hat one cannot,
another can.

William Davenant

❀

*W*hile the right friends
are near us, we feel that all is well.
Our everyday life blossoms suddenly
into bright possibilities.

Helen Keller

*W*e is terrific.
Diana Ross

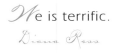

*P*eople must believe
in each other, and feel
that it can be done and
must be done; in that way
they are enormously strong.
We must keep up each
other's courage.

Vincent van Gogh

*T*hank you for
believing in me before
I believed in myself.

Kobi Yamada

❀

*S*ometimes our light goes out
but is blown into flame by another
human being. Each of us owes
deepest thanks to those who
have rekindled this light.

Albert Schweitzer

*E*verywhere, we learn best
from those whom we love.

Goethe

❋

*S*omeone saw
something in you once.
That's partly why you are
where you are today. Whoever
it was had the kindness and the
foresight to bet on your future.
Today, take 10 minutes to write a
grateful note to the person who
helped you. You'll keep a
wonderful friendship alive.

Harry Gray

There are people who
take the heart out of you,
and there are people who
put it back.

Elizabeth David

❋

Why, I don't know—but,
I always like myself better when
I'm with my friends. Somehow,
they pull the best from me,
effortlessly, weightlessly.

Jeri Burnett

*P*erhaps friendship is
the process of my leading you
gently back to yourself.

Saint-Empery

*T*o love a person is
to learn the song that
is in their heart, and to
sing it to them when they
have forgotten.

Thomas Chandler

*W*e all need to be
recognized for what we're doing,
for our work. Every once in a while
we need someone to come up to us
and say, "You're beautiful. That was
well done. That's nice."

Leo Buscaglia

❁

*T*here is only one real deprivation,
I decided this morning, and that is
not to be able to give one's gifts
to those one loves most.

May Sarton

*M*oreover, in loving
their friend they love what
is good for themselves.

Aristotle

❁

*I*t's a great satisfaction
knowing that for a brief point in time
you made a difference.

Irene Natividad

❁

*W*e are rich only
through what we give,
and poor only through
what we refuse.

Ann-Sophie Swetchine

*P*eople who love us
for what we are, not for what
we have done, are precious support
when we're trying to do and be more.

Peter McWilliams

❀

I love you, not only
for what you are, but for
what I am when I am with you.
I love you, not only for what
you have made of yourself, but for
what you are making of me.

Roy Croft

*A*ll we have to do
to be successful is follow the
advice we give others.

Dear Abby

❀

*N*othing is so embarrassing as
watching your friend do something
you told him couldn't be done.

Calvin Peete

❀

*I*f at first you don't succeed,
you'll probably have more friends.

Whoopi Goldberg

One can't really play
with her friends in a tiara.

Princess Diana

✿

The worst part of success
is to try to find someone who
is happy for you.

Bette Midler

✿

If I'm such a legend,
why am I so lonely?

Judy Garland

*W*inning has always
meant much to me, but winning
friends has meant the most.

Babe Didrikson Zaharias

❁

*T*o laugh often and much,
to win the respect of intelligent
people and the affection of children…
to leave the world a bit better…
to know even one life had breathed
easier because you have lived,
that is to have succeeded.

Ralph Waldo Emerson

*K*eep shining,
my bright and shining star of a friend.
Ivy Baker

❀

*G*row into your perfection.
Kobi Yamada

❀

*N*ever let anyone steal your dream.
It's your dream, not theirs!
Dan Zadra

A friend
walks in
when the whole world
walks out.
Walter Winchell

You've got a friend™

In prosperity our friends know us;
in adversity we know our friends.

J. Churton Collins

❀

Lots of people want to ride
with you in the limo, but what
you want is someone who will
take the bus with you when
the limo breaks down.

Oprah Winfrey

❀

Some people we can always depend
upon for making the best, instead of the
worst, of whatever happens.

Sandra Wilde

*L*ove is what you've
been through with somebody.

James Thurber

❀

*W*e have been friends together
in sunshine and shade.

Caroline Norton

❀

I didn't know,
until I was at odds with the world,
how much my friends who believe
in me…mean to me.

D. H. Lawrence

You've got a friend™

Crises does not make friends,
it reveals them.
Don Ward

❀

The object is not to
see through one another, but
to see one another through.
Peter DeVries

❀

Friendship is two hearts
pulling at one load.
Dan Zadra

48

You've got a friend™

"*That* would be nice."

Charlie Brown,
on hearing that in life you win some and lose some

How can there be so much
difference between a day off
and an off day?

Doug Larson

My friend Betsy will say,
'I don't know whose life I hate more—
yours or mine.' It makes us laugh.

Francine Russo

We might as well live.
Dorothy Parker

❋

Since the house is on fire
let us warm ourselves.

Italian saying

❋

If you're already walking on thin ice,
why not dance?

Gil Atkinson

You've got a friend™

The world knows nothing
of its greatest people.
Henry Taylor

❀

It's the friends you can call up
at 4 A.M. that matter.
Marlene Dietrich

❀

I could do without
many things with no hardship—
you are not one of them.
Ashleigh Brilliant

51

Friendship
glows in the dark.
Cat Lane

❀

Trouble is a part of life,
and if you don't share it, you don't give
the person who loves you a chance
to love you enough.
Dinah Shore

❀

People say I've had a hard life,
but I've also had very good
company along the way.
Helen Keller

Nothing lasts forever,
not even your troubles.

Mileposts

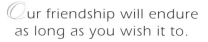

Our friendship will endure
as long as you wish it to.

Barbara Armand

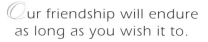

The hard times
we go through will lead to
the good times we'll have.

Henry Littlefield

$\mathcal{I}$ think
we're here
for each other.

Carol Burnett

The best thing
to hold onto in life
is each other.

Audrey Hepburn

Some people make the world
more special just by being in it.

Kelly Ann Rothaus

'Twas her thinking of others
made you think of her.

Elizabeth Barrett Browning

$\mathcal{C}$aring is everything.

❀

$\mathcal{T}$reasure the one
who thinks of you when all others
are thinking of themselves.

James Ginn

❀

$\mathcal{I}$t is lovely,
when I forget all birthdays,
including my own, to find that
somebody remembers me.

Ellen Glasgow

When friends ask,
there is no tomorrow…
only now.

Alexander Drey

❁

If a friend is in trouble,
don't annoy him by asking if
there is anything you can do.
Make up something appropriate
and do it!

Edgar Howe

Go ahead and cry,
I'll catch your tears.

Jilleen Russell

The love of our friend in all its fullness
simply means being able to say to him,
"What are you going through?"

Simone Weil

Measure your friends
around the heart.

English Proverb

*F*or many people in this world,
life is cold, lonely and hard. If they had
one friend, their lives would not only
be different, but happier. In the plan of
God, a friendship is a touch of heaven
on earth. And we can all bring a touch
of heaven into someone's life.

Rev. Mark Connolly

❀

*I*f someone listens,
or stretches out a hand, or whispers
a kind word of encouragement, or
attempts to understand, extraordinary
things begin to happen.

Loretta Girzartis

When I take you in my life,
I now have four arms instead of two.
Two heads. Four legs. Two possibilities
for joy. Sure, two possibilities for tears,
but I can be there for you while you cry
and you can be there while I cry,
because nobody should ever cry alone.

Leo Buscaglia

❋

Each of us stands alone in this vast
world, momentarily bathed in a ray
of sunlight. And suddenly it's night.
If you stand together with me, we can
share the sunlight, and believe me,
the night won't seem so frightening.

Quasimodo

And remember, we all
stumble, every one of us.
That's why it's a comfort
to go hand in hand.

Emily Kimbrough

❃

Lean on me
when you're not strong,
and I'll be your friend,
I'll help you carry on,
for it won't be long
till I'm going to need
somebody to lean on.

Bill Withers

*A*h! How good it feels,
the hand of an old friend.

Longfellow

❀

*W*hen someone hugs you,
let them be the first to let go.

H. Jackson Brown

❀

*H*ow beautiful it is to be able
to say to someone, "I need you."
We think to be a grownup we must be
independent and not need anyone—and
that's why we're all dying of loneliness!
How wonderful to be needed!

Leo Buscaglia

*O*ur greatest duty and our
main duty is to help others, and please,
if you can't help them, would you
please not hurt them?

Dalai Lama

*W*hat could I have done
to have saved someone in my life?

Arthur Miller

*T*ake good care of yourself,
just as you have taken such good
care of others.

Dan Zadra

*W*e will
always have time for the
things we put first.

Liane Steele

Let us pause to warm
our hands before the fire of life.

Who puts the coffee on for two.
Who makes me laugh when I am blue.
No matter what I have to do—
My friend, there's always time for you.

Unknown

No day ends if it makes a memory.

*Y*ou must be present to win.

Reminder usually made at raffles

❁

*N*o matter what troubles or
travails may loom ahead for you,
do not let yourself be cheated
out of the joy and beauty of today.

Henry Ward Beecher

❁

*N*o one has time;
we have to make time.

James Rhoen

*N*obody sees a flower really;
it is so small. We haven't time,
and to see takes time—like to
have a friend takes time.

Georgia O'Keeffe

❀

*W*hen just being together is
more important than what you do,
you are with a friend.

Stephanie James

❀

*S*he took me to lunch even when
I wasn't tax deductible.

Reminiscences

You've got a friend™

*W*e don't recognize the most
significant moments in our lives
until they are past us.

Moonlight Graham,
"Field of Dreams"

✿

I would rather have 30 minutes
of 'wonderful' than a lifetime of
nothing special.

Julia Roberts

✿

*O*pen your mind, open your heart,
open your arms, take it all in.

Kobi Yamada

The best way to pay for
a lovely moment is to enjoy it.

Richard Bach

In the end, what affects your
life most deeply are things too
simple to talk about.

Nell Blaine

Hold out your hands
to feel the luxury of the sunbeams.

Helen Keller

*T*here's no time
like the pleasant.

Oliver Herford

❁

*T*he greatest lesson from the mystics
is that the sacred is in the ordinary,
that it is to be found in one's daily life,
in one's neighbors, friends, and family,
in one's back yard.

Abraham H. Maslow

❁

*C*ount each day a separate life.

Seneca

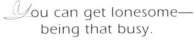

You've got a friend™

You can get lonesome—
being that busy.

Isabel Lennart

For the sake of making a living
we forget to live.

Margaret Fuller

Work is the greatest thing
in the world. So you should save
some of it for tomorrow.

Don Herold

71

I shall tell you a great secret,
my friend. Do not wait for the last
judgment, it takes place every day.

Albert Camus

❋

We really need only
five things on this earth:
Some food, some sun, some work,
some fun and someone.

Beatrice Nolan

❋

*N*othing is worth more
than this day.

Goethe

People are
more fun than
anybody.

Dorothy Parker

*L*ife is a lot more amusing
than we thought.

Andrew Lang

❀

*T*hat is the best—to laugh
with someone because you both think
the same things are funny.

Gloria Vanderbilt

❀

*L*aughter is
the best communion of all.

Robert Fulghum

There are souls in this world
who have the gift of finding joy
everywhere—and leaving it
behind them when they go.

Faber

❀

It's hard to imagine things without
her, you know, because every now and
then it's like, you know, I've gotta hear
that laugh that she does. I've just gotta
hear that. It's like craving your
favorite food or something.

The Friends Network

*L*ife is too important
to be taken seriously.

Oscar Wilde

✿

*A*nything worth taking seriously
is worth making fun of.

Tom Lehrer

✿

*I*t is bad to suppress laughter.
It goes back down and spreads
to your hips.

Fred Allen

The joy of living
was meant to be shared.
Happiness was born a twin.
Don Ward

Take time every day
to do something ridiculous.
Philipa Walker

Life is too short to be cranky.
Beej Whiteaker-Hawks

*P*rocrastination is fun.
Just wait and see.

Graffito

❁

*H*ow beautiful it is to do nothing,
and then to rest afterward.

Spanish proverb

❁

*W*hen you start to look like
your passport picture—you know
you need a vacation.

Falon James

I finally figured out the
main reason to be alive is to enjoy it.

Rita Mae Brown

*W*e're always being told
that time is running out; it is and
getting things done won't stop it.

Joan Silber

*T*here's never enough time
to do all the nothing you want.

Bill Watterson

*B*oredom arises from routine.
Joy, wonder, rapture, arise from
surprise. Routine leads to boredom
and if we are bored, we are boring.

Leo Buscaglia

❀

*K*eep smiling—It makes
people wonder what you're up to.

Bob Dolfay

❀

*E*njoy yourself.
If you can't enjoy yourself,
enjoy someone else.

Jack Schaefer

$\mathcal{W}$e have
one thing in common.
Each of us brings to our
lives a certain amount
of mess.

Francis Coppola

*M*y friend is not perfect,
no more than I,
and so we suit each other
admirably.

Alexander Pope

❁

I've only met four
perfect people in my life and
I didn't like any of them.

Dorothy Parker

It isn't easy being green.
Kermit the Frog

A friend is someone
you want to be around when
you feel like being by yourself.
Nancy Knowland

A friend is someone
so there's no more need
to be normal.
Ashleigh Brilliant

*Y*ou're never too old to learn,
but many people keep putting it off.

Graffito

❀

*I*n college, all my
friends drank deeply at the
fountain of knowledge.
I just gargled.

Totie Fields

❀

*B*eing with Mary was like being
in a telephone booth with an open
umbrella—no matter which way you
turned, you got it in the eye.

Jean Kerr

84

One out of four people
in this country is mentally imbalanced.
Think of your three closest friends.
If they seem okay, then you're the one.

Gehrhart Landers

❀

I love you no matter what you do,
but do you have to do so much of it?

Jean Illsley Clarke

❀

I'm nuts and they all know it.
But, because we grew up together,
they understand why I turned out so
wacky. To them, I'll always be a friend
first, and a clown second. That's gold.

Denny Girault, comedian

Experience is the
mistakes we like to remember.

Berta Sklansky

❁

God has put up with a lot
from most of us.

Colette

❁

We seldom make the
same mistake twice. Usually it's three
times or more.

Marilyn Grey

Thanks for
teaching me
right from wrong…
I especially liked
the 'wrong' part.

M.D. O'Conner

My friend is someone
who helps me get in trouble.

Jimmy, Age 7

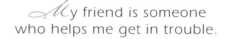

Perhaps the straight and
narrow path would be wider if
more of my friends used it.

Kay Ingram

Lead me not into temptation;
I can find the way myself.

Rita Mae Brown

You've got a friend™

I spend way too much time
searching through the Bible
for loopholes.

W.C. Fields

❀

*O*n the whole, human beings
want to be good, but not too good
and not quite all the time.

George Orwell

❀

*I*t's been my experience that folks
who have no vices have very few virtues.

Abraham Lincoln

Life is a banquet and most
poor fools are starving to death.

Auntie Mame

I hate to eat and eat and
eat and run.

Neila Ross

I like Hostess fruit pies.
She prefers pop-up toaster tarts because
they don't require so much cooking.

Carrie Snow

*V*eni, vidi, Visa.
(We came, we saw, we went shopping.)

Jan Barrett

❀

*W*e do not spend all our time
buying things; we spend part of it
taking them back.

Edgar Watson Howe

❀

*M*y friends buy just as many wigs
and makeup things as I do. They just
don't wear them all at the same time.

Dolly Parton

*T*he trouble with trouble is
that it always starts out like fun.

James Thurber

❋

*O*pportunity knocks only once,
but temptation bangs on
the door for years.

Frank Vizarre

❋

*N*o one is ever old enough
to know better.

Holbrook Jackson

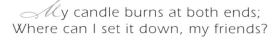
My candle burns at both ends;
Where can I set it down, my friends?

Richard Armour

✻

The trouble with resisting temptation is
that you may not get another chance.

Laurence J. Peter

✻

No, you never get any fun
out of the things you haven't done.

Ogden Nash

$\mathcal{P}$lead guilty
and often to
loving your family
and friends.

Dan Zadra

*L*ove is nothing more than
massive liking.

Jim Cecil

❀

*T*he verb 'to love' in Persian is
'to have a friend.' 'I love you' translated
literally is 'I have you as a friend,' and
'I don't like you' simply means
'I don't have you as a friend.'

Shusha Guppy

❀

*T*o love anyone is nothing else
than to wish that person good.

St. Thomas Aquinas

95

*L*oving someone allows you
to see him as God intended him.

Fyodor Dostoyevsky

❀

*T*here are many compliments
that may come to an individual in
the course of a lifetime, but there is
no higher tribute than to be loved
by those who know us best.

Rev. Dale E. Turner

❀

*I*nsomuch as any one
pushes you nearer to God,
he or she is your friend.

French Proverb

We are taught there are seven
sacraments, but some theologians
say there should be eight.
The eighth sacrament is the
"sacrament of friendship."

Rev. Mark Connolly

❋

In India, every time you
meet somebody, you put your hands
in front and say, 'Namaste.' That means,
'I honor the place in you where the
entire universe resides. I honor the
place in you where, if you are at that
place in you and I am at that place
in me, there is only one of us.'

Leo Buscaglia

We make our friends;
we make our enemies; but God
sends our next door neighbors.

G. K. Chesterton

As neighbors we began by
simply chatting over the hedge;
then one of us would squeeze
through an opening in the branches.
Eventually we'd carved out a small door
in the leaves. Rather than walking
around front to the path, one of us
would ritually crouch and crawl
through to discuss the weather
and our dreams.

Kathryn Livingston

You've got a friend™

There's something special
about a next-door neighbor—
about looking into their house at night
(not as a spy!) and seeing their
shapes moving. The presence of
my good neighbors was a comfort;
their daily comings and goings
served as a friendly counterpoint to
my own hectic schedule, and I knew
that whatever problem I might
encounter during the day
(however large or small it might be),
I could count on them for help.

Kathryn Livingston

99

The scariest thing about middle age is that we know we're going to grow out of it.

Marcie M. Kinney

I'm 53 now, my little kids are all grown up, and I am a writer. But running has stayed the same. Each morning, into the snows of January, the suns of July, despite creaking joints and bouts of menopausal insomnia, my friends and I run together. It's not that we love running so much. It's that we love each other.

Cristina Negron

*A*h, but there is no friend
like a sister.

Christina Rossetti, 1862

❋

*D*ear Norma:
Am sending you twenty-five dollars.
It's going to be hard, baby—we'll probably
want money pretty bad pretty often—but
no unworthy girl ever had so many friends
as I have, and we shan't starve, because
we can borrow. I'm as crazy to see you
as if I were going to be married to you—
no one is such good pals as we are.

Edna St. Vincent Millay

inviting her sister Norma to join her in Greenwich Village

I told you it would happen,
that our friendship was bound to end.
Although I know you care,
I cannot consider you as a friend.
Please don't try to argue,
just try to understand
that time can change people,
as the tide can change the sand.
Our friendship has been lovely,
but you see it has an end.
For now I fell in a different way,
I've fallen in love with you my friend.

Kyra, "My Friend,"
The Friendship Page

*P*latonic friendship is
the interval between the
introduction and the first kiss.

Sophie Loeb

*C*ame but for friendship
and took away love.

Thomas Moore

*F*unny, the biggest commitment
to friendship we can make is
sealed with just two little words:
"I do."

Steve Potter

103

*I*f I were to marry again tomorrow,
I wouldn't give up one friend. I'd take
them all with me as a sort of dowry and
tell my new husband that he was
getting a rich wife.

Merle Shain

❋

*T*he truth is,
friendship is every bit as sacred
and eternal as marriage.

Katherine Mansfield

We have a great deal
more friendship than is
ever spoken. How many
persons we meet in houses,
whom yet we honor,
and who will honor us!
How many we see in the street,
or sit with in church, whom,
though silently, we warmly
rejoice to be with.
Read the language of these
wandering eye-beams.
The heart knoweth.

Ralph Waldo Emerson

Friendship is
rhythm.
Also blues.

Count Basie

*F*riends do not live
in harmony, merely, as some say,
but in melody.

Henry David Thoreau

❋

*T*rue friendship is seldom serene.

Madame De Sevigne

❋

*W*e may not always see eye to eye,
but we can try to see heart to heart.

Sam Levenson

*S*ometimes it's worse to win a fight
than to lose.

Billie Holiday

❀

*S*ticks and stones may break our bones,
but words will still break our hearts.

Robert Fulghum

❀

*M*isery is when your
very best friend calls you a name
she really didn't mean to call you at all.
Misery is when you call your very best
friend a name you didn't mean
to call her, either.

Langston Hughes

You've got a friend™

*G*ood friend, always be open
to the miracle of the second chance.

Rev. David Stier

❀

*W*e could be friends
Like friends are supposed to be.
You, picking up the telephone
Calling me
to come over and play,
or take a walk,
finding a place, to sit and talk
Or just goof around
Like friends do,
Me, picking up the telephone
Calling you.

Myra Cohn Livingston

You've got a friend™

*F*orgiveness is the act
of admitting we are like our friends.

Christina Baldwin

✿

I bear no grudges.
My heart is as big as the sky
and I have a mind that retains
absolutely nothing.

Bette Midler

✿

*W*e would like to start from scratch.
Where is scratch?

Elias Canetti

No one can go back and make
a brand new start,
But anyone can start from here and
make a brand new end.

Reminiscences

The future is
sending back good wishes and
waiting with open arms.

Kobi Yamada

People change and forget
to tell each other.

Lillian Hellman

❀

It doesn't happen all at once.
You become. It takes a long time.

Margery Williams

❀

The most beautiful
discovery true friends make is
that they can grow separately
without growing apart.

Elisabeth Foley

*D*on't be dismayed at good-byes.
A farewell is necessary before you
can meet again. And meeting again,
after moments or lifetimes, is certain
for those who are friends.

Richard Bach

❁

A part of you has grown in me
And so you see, it's you and me
Together forever and never apart,
Maybe in distance,
But never in heart.

Unknown

You've got a friend™

I Feel So Miserable Without You,
It's Almost Like Having You Here.
Song Title by Stephen Bishop

The one good thing about
not seeing you is that I can
write you letters.
Svetlana Allilnyeva

Just put a little of
yourself in the evelope,
seal it up and send it off!
Dan Zadra

$\mathcal{A}$nd the song,
from beginning to end,
I found in the heart
of a friend.

Henry Wadsworth Longfellow

*W*e two are friends,
tells everything.
Unknown

✾

*E*lizabeth Barrett Browning:
"What is the secret of your life?
Tell me, that I may make mine
beautiful, too."
Charles Kingsley: "I had a friend."

God evidently does not
intend us all to be rich, or powerful
or great, but He does intend us all
to be friends.

Ralph Waldo Emerson

❋

Who, being loved, is poor?

Oscar Wilde

❋

I awoke this morning with
devout thanksgiving for my friends,
the old and the new. I call God
'Beautiful' for these gifts.

Ralph Waldo Emerson

I just got old
and couldn't help it.

Jean Calment, age 117

❋

*C*ount your nights by stars,
not shadows.
Count your days by smiles, not tears.
And on any birthday morning,
Count your age by friends,
not years.

Unknown

They were such close friends that
even when they were two worn-out
old people, they kept on…playing
together like half-crazy puppies.

Unknown

❋

The two old men sit in silence together,
relishing memories of the past. They are
lifelong friends and need no words to share
their thoughts. One quavers to the other:
'May you live a hundred years, and may
I live ninety-nine.' The other nods his old
white head and gravely says: 'Let us go
home together and drink a cup a wine.'

Han Chi, "Old Friends"

In our dreams
we are never eighty.
Anne Sexton

There may be snow on the roof,
but there's still a fire in the fireplace.
George Burns

There may be snow on the roof,
but there's still a fire in the fireplace.
George Burns

We are not growing older, we are
just becoming more concentrated.
Karen Wick

*I*f you want
a thing done well, get a couple
of old broads to do it.

Bette Midler

❀

*L*ady Astor, age 89,
planning her 90th birthday party:
'And there will be dancing!
I, for one, intend to
dance 'til dawn.'

Reminiscences

I'll never be a big wheel,
or a great lover, or a terrific athlete,
or a gourmet cook, or a community
leader. But one thing I can be
is a really good friend.

Dave MacNee

*D*ear George: Remember
no man is a failure
who has friends.
Thanks for the wings!
Love, Clarence.

Clarence, the Angel

"It's A Wonderful Life"

Treasure each other in
the recognition that we do not know
how long we will have each other.

Joshua Liebman

❀

I cannot forgive my
friends for dying; I do not find
these vanishing acts of theirs
at all amusing.

Logan Pearsall Smith

❀

If you should die before me,
ask if you could bring a friend.

Stone Temple Pilots

I shall live because there
are a few people I want
to stay with for the longest
possible time.

A. J. Salih

Someday I would like to
stand on the moon with my best friend,
look down through a quarter of a million
miles of space and say, 'There certainly is
a beautiful earth out tonight.'

Lt. Colonel W. H. Rankin

You've got a friend™

I seek, dear friend, my heart's true wish to send you, that you may know, that far or near my loving thoughts attend you.

Wisdom of the Heart

❀

For this I bless you most. You give much and know not that you give at all.

Kahlil Gibran

125

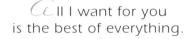

All I want for you
is the best of everything.

Veronica Lake
Letter to a childhood friend

❀

The good you do is not lost
though you forget it.

Jiri Masala

❀

And could I have but one
wish this year, this only it would be:
I'd like to be the sort of friend
that you have been to me.

Edgar Guest

When I count
my blessings,
I count you
twice.

Irish Proverb

Also available from Compendium Publishing are these spirited and compelling companion books of great quotations.

Because of You™
Celebrating the Difference You Make™
Thoughts to Inspire the People Who Inspire Us™

Brilliance™
Uncommon Voices From Uncommon Women™
Thoughts to Inspire and Celebrate Your Achievements™

Forever Remembered™
A Gift for the Grieving Heart™
Cherished messages of hope, love and comfort from
courageous people who have lost a loved one.™

I Believe in You™
To your heart, your dream and the difference you make.

Little Miracles™
To renew your dreams, lift your spirits, and strengthen your resolve.™
Cherished messages of hope, joy, love, kindness and courage.™

Reach for the Stars™
Give up the Good to Go for the Great.™

Thank You™
In appreciation of you, and all that you do.™

To Your Success™
Dream • Team • Care • Dare™
Thoughts to Give Wings to Your Work and Your Dreams™

Whatever It Takes™
A Journey into the Heart of Human Achievement™
Thoughts to Inspire and Celebrate Your Commitment to Excellence™

These books may be ordered directly from the publisher (800) 914-3327.
But please try your bookstore first!

www.compendiuminc.com